Dealing With Waste

LEFTOVER FOOD

Sally Morgan

W
FRANKLIN WATTS
LONDON•SYDNEY

First published in 2006 by
Franklin Watts
338 Euston Road,
London NW1 3BH

Franklin Watts Australia
Hachette Children's Books
Level 17/207 Kent Street,
Sydney NSW 2000

Produced for Franklin Watts by White-Thomson Publishing Ltd
210 High Street,
Lewes BN7 2NH

Editor: Rachel Minay
Designer: Brenda Cole
Picture research: Morgan Interactive Ltd
Consultant: Graham Williams

Picture credits:
The publishers would like to thank the following for reproducing these photographs:
Alamy 11 (Jim West), 22 (Mark Boulton); Brand X/Imagestate 10; Ecoscene front cover
top right (Kevin King), 6 (Sally Morgan), 7 (Christine Osborne), 8 (Sally Morgan), 9
(Christine Osborne), 12 (Jamie Harron), 13 (Tom Ennis), 14 (Sally Morgan), 15 (Alan
Towse), 16 (Robert Pickett), 17 (Christine Osborne), 18 (Sally Morgan), 19 (Alan
Towse), 20 (Christine Osborne), 21 (Sally Morgan); Kari Erik Marttila Photography
front cover bottom right (Kari Marttila); Recyclenow.com front cover main image.

Every attempt has been made to clear copyright. Should there
be any inadvertent omission please apply to the publisher for rectification.

British Library Cataloguing in Publication Data
A CIP catalogue record for this book
is available from the British Library.

ISBN-10: 0 7496 6433 9
ISBN-13: 978 0 7496 6433 6

Dewey classification: 363.72'88

Printed in China

Contents

Food for all

There are more than 6 billion people living on Earth.
The number is increasing every day. By 2025 there may
be as many as 8.5 billion people. All these people need food.
However, the world's food supply is not shared out equally.

Shops full of food

In developed countries there is plenty of food. The shops are full
of food from all over the world and food is much cheaper than
ever before. There is also lots of food waste, as people eat what
they want and throw away the rest. Much of the food is wrapped
in packaging, which creates even more waste.

There are plenty of fruits and vegetables
for sale at this floating market outside
Bangkok in Thailand.

Going hungry

In contrast, in many developing countries people cannot grow enough food so it is in short supply. The shelves in the shops are empty and often people rely on food provided by aid agencies and charities to feed their families.

Did you know...?

Every single day around 25,000 people die because they do not have enough food to eat or through some other hunger-related cause. Sadly, three out of four of all these deaths are children under five years old.

These villagers live in an extremely dry area of Ethiopia. They are preparing the ground to sow their seeds. However, if the rains do not come the crops will fail.

It's my world!

Think about how much food you eat each day. Do you throw any away? Sometimes food travels many miles from the place where it is grown to where it is eaten. Look at the labels on the food you eat. Where did it come from?

Did you know...?

As much as one-third of the food produced in some developed countries is thrown away.

Wasting food

Have a look in your rubbish bin. How much of the rubbish is food or food packaging? On average, as much as 35% of household rubbish comes from the kitchen or garden.

These tomatoes have been dumped beside a road in Tenerife. There is nothing wrong with them but the farmer cannot sell them and so has thrown them away.

Why is food thrown away?

People throw away food for all sorts of reasons. Food is left on plates or in packaging, or it is thrown away because it is not wanted or liked. Sometimes food goes mouldy and is no longer fit to be eaten. Sometimes food is thrown away because it is past its 'use-by' date and might be unsafe to eat. Farmers, shops and supermarkets throw away food that they have been unable to sell.

This woman is sorting out food donations that will be given to needy people living in Detroit, USA.

Did you know...?

Restaurants and other places that serve food can make small changes to reduce the amount of waste they produce. For example, they can use reusable plates and utensils rather than disposable ones and they can serve sauces, salt, pepper and sugar in large dispensers rather than individual packets. They can also use washable cloths rather than disposable ones.

Landfills and incinerators

Usually, waste food is placed in large containers or skips and taken to landfill sites or incinerators. Landfill sites are large holes in the ground where rubbish is buried. These holes are usually created by quarrying companies that dig gravel and rock from the ground. Incinerators are places where rubbish is burnt. Sometimes the heat from burning the rubbish is used to generate electricity.

Food donations

Many supermarkets and other food businesses donate food that is past its sell-by date but before its use-by date to charities. This may include tinned food and packets of cereals. These charities give the food to the needy. Sometimes the food is sent overseas as emergency aid to feed people after natural disasters such as tsunamis and earthquakes. Food donations help to reduce the amount of food that is burnt or ends up in landfill sites.

Attracting pests

All sorts of animals are attracted to food waste.
If food is left in dustbins or simply put in plastic bags
on the ground, it is soon discovered by animals.

Urban animals

Rats and mice are often the first to find
food waste but large animals, such as foxes
and even badgers, look for food waste, too.
Animals that live in urban areas have learnt
that food is often left on the streets and
have come to rely on it as a source of food.
Foxes and badgers turn over dustbins and
rip open bags in their search, emptying
rubbish over the street, while rats and mice
gnaw holes in bags. Birds such as gulls,
crows and jackdaws also feed on scraps
of food on the street.

Did you know...?

New York is trying to reduce the number
of rats in the city. It is estimated that
there are as many as 8 rats for every
person living in the city, which means
a massive 64 million rats in total. In the
year 2000, more than 13 million dollars
(over 7 million pounds) were spent trying
to exterminate the rats. But less waste on
the streets could mean fewer rats.

Bears, such as this American black
bear, are a common sight around
rubbish dumps in many parts of North
America where they search through
the bags of waste looking for food.

The large quantities of food that are thrown away attract huge flocks of gulls to landfill sites.

Flies and cockroaches

Flies are attracted to waste food, too. They gather around bags of waste food and bins on the street and come into kitchens and factories. They lay their eggs on the waste food and the eggs hatch into maggots. The maggots feed on the food and within a few days they pupate and turn into adult flies.

Flies land on all sorts of surfaces such as animal droppings and rubbish so they may carry bacteria that cause disease. All food preparation areas have to be protected from flies.

Cockroaches emerge at night to feed on food crumbs on the floor. They like warm, humid places such as kitchens and cellars.

It's my world!

How clean is your kitchen? Are there any food crumbs on the floor or inside cupboards that could attract pests? Have a look behind your cooker and under your refrigerator. You may be surprised and horrified by the amount of food you find!

Composting food

Food is made up of organic matter. Organic matter is made by living organisms and it is a material that will break down naturally. This means it is easy to recycle.

Once a fresh layer of garden waste has been tipped onto a compost heap it is covered with a lid or an old piece of carpet. This traps in the heat given off by the decaying waste.

Compost heaps

One of the best places to dispose of food waste is on a compost heap. Here, the waste can break down and form a compost that can be used on the soil in gardens. Even paper plates and paper packaging can be put on a compost heap along with garden waste.

Compost heaps range in size from small containers in the garden to huge commercial ones that are designed to break down large volumes of food and garden waste. As the waste breaks down it releases lots of heat. It gets hot in the middle of the compost and this kills any harmful bacteria that may be present in the food. The resulting compost is full of nutrients and this can be added to the soil to help plants grow. Compost is often sold in bags to gardeners.

Quick turnaround

Composting can take weeks or months, depending on how much air and moisture the compost receives. Also, leaves and food break down more quickly than paper plates and cardboard. If it is turned regularly and there is plenty of air, compost can be made in just 12 weeks. It takes longer to make compost in winter because the cold weather slows the process down. If the compost becomes wet and slimy it is because too much soft material (such as grass clippings and vegetable peelings) has been added. This can be overcome by adding chopped-up twigs, wood chips and some shredded or crumpled newspaper to give the compost a better texture.

Saving money

Some supermarket chains have their own composting facilities to dispose of food waste. This is an environmentally friendly method, as the nutrients are recycled rather than wasted.

The Netherlands, Austria and Germany compost almost half of their organic waste. The UK only manages to compost about 4%. In the USA just over 7% of organic waste in rubbish is composted.

It's my world!

What can be composted?

- Lawn clippings
- Leaves
- Shredded stalks and hedge clippings
- Cut flowers
- Vegetable and fruit scraps
- Fallen apples and other fruits
- Teabags, tea leaves and coffee grounds
- Eggshells
- Newspaper.

What cannot be composted?

- Diseased plants
- Plastics, glass and other non-organic materials
- Cooked food including meat and fish
- Raw meat and fish, dairy produce, eggs
- Some weeds (such as nettles, bindweed, ground elder)
- Coloured glossy paper
- Pet droppings.

Natural recycling

Compost heaps mimic natural processes. If you walk through a wood in autumn you will see a layer of leaves on the woodland floor. By summer most of these have disappeared. This is because they have been broken down.

Decomposers

Decomposers are organisms that are responsible for recycling dead animal bodies, animal droppings and plant matter. Among the larger decomposers are the earthworms, beetles and flies. Flies lay their eggs on dead bodies and the eggs hatch into maggots that feed on the dead bodies. The larger decomposers break up the dead matter into smaller pieces, which are food for micro-organisms, such as fungi and bacteria. The decomposition releases nutrients back into the soil so they can be used again by plants.

Snails eat dead and decaying vegetation on the ground. They grind up the vegetation using their rough tongue, which is called a radula.

It's my world!

Some leaves take longer to break down than others. You can see which break down the quickest by collecting lots of different types of leaves, placing them in a mesh bag (such as those used to package fruits) and burying the bag in the ground. Leave the bag in the ground for several months and then dig it up. See which leaves have broken down the most.

Autumn fungi

Fungi are important decomposers. Most of them live in the ground out of sight, but they can be seen in autumn when they grow above ground to form toadstools. The job of the toadstool is to produce and release millions of spores which are carried away by the wind. When a spore lands it grows into a new fungus.

These bracket fungi are growing on an old tree stump. They are feeding on the wood that makes up the stump.

Wormeries

Worms are great for breaking down food waste. It is possible to buy or build compost bins that are suitable for keeping a large number of special worms. They are called wormeries.

Vermiculture

Using worms to break down waste is called vermiculture. Vermiculture is becoming increasingly popular around the world as a means of breaking down food and animal waste.

Special compost bins are set up and filled with worms that break down the food into a compost. This can take just four weeks so the process is much quicker than a traditional compost bin. The food waste is turned into compost that can be used in gardens. As the food is broken down, a liquid is produced. This is full of nutrients so it can be used as a fertilizer on plants.

Large-scale wormeries are built to dispose of commercial food waste. In countries such as India and Pakistan, villagers dig pits about 3 m long and 1 m deep in which they dispose of organic waste and allow the worms to break it down. The compost that is formed is used to improve soil on farms.

This wormery is made up of several layers. Food scraps are put into the top layer. As the food is broken down by the worms a new layer is added and compost is removed from the bottom one.

Worms do not like the light so they are found a few centimetres below the surface of the compost where it is warm, damp and dark.

Did you know...?

The benefits of a wormery are:

▸ less food waste remains in the rubbish

▸ it is ideal for people with small gardens

▸ it produces a liquid fertilizer for house and garden plants

▸ the compost that is left behind is great for putting on soil.

Hungry worms

Wormeries use a special type of worm that is smaller than the common earthworm you find in the garden. They are called tiger or brandling worms and they are small red worms that have an enormous appetite. Some worms are able to eat their own weight in food each day. Tiger worms grow quickly, reaching an adult length of about 7 cm in just 6 weeks or less. They can live for up to two years.

Food for animals

In many parts of the world, families living in rural areas keep animals. The animals supply them with a source of milk, meat and eggs. Food waste can be fed to the animals.

Recycling food

Food waste can be recycled if it is fed to animals such as chickens and pigs. Chickens eat a variety of foods and will peck over food from the kitchen as well as fallen fruit and misshapen vegetables. Food waste from shops and food manufacturers can be sent to farms as animal food, too. For example, local bakeries often have arrangements with local farmers who collect all the stale bread and feed it to pigs and poultry. However, care must be taken that the food does not contain any meat. Animals are not allowed to eat meat products in case diseases such as foot-and-mouth or BSE are transmitted from one animal to another.

Chickens are a common sight on farms all around the world, such as this one in Ghana. Chickens provide the farmer with a supply of eggs and meat.

Pigs will eat almost all types of plant and happily feed on vegetable scraps from the kitchen or garden.

It's my world!

Some food waste is safe to put out for wild birds. Leftovers that you can put on a bird table include:

▸ stale bread

▸ biscuits and stale cake

▸ fat from meat

▸ leftover cereals

▸ bruised apples.

Processing waste food

There are problems with feeding waste food to animals because the content of the waste varies a lot from day to day and this is not good for the animals. To overcome this, waste food is processed into small pellets that can be fed to animals. The nutrient content of the pellets is easier to control and farmers can weigh out a certain amount of food each day. During the process of making the pellets, the food is heated to high temperatures and this kills any bacteria that could harm the animals.

Food into new products

Food-processing factories, restaurants and fast-food outlets use a lot of cooking oil and this often ends up in drains and sewers. As the fat builds up, it can completely block a pipe. Waste fat should be recycled rather than thrown away.

Reducing oil waste

Commercial kitchens use a lot of cooking oil. This may be liquid oil or solid in the form of lard and margarine. They can reduce the amount they use in a number of ways, which in turn reduces the amount of waste. Cooking oil that is used for deep fat frying need not be replaced after it has been used just once. Often it can be reused a few times before it has to be replaced. Any oil that has to be replaced should be put in a large container so that it can be collected and recycled. It should not be tipped down the drain!

It's my world!

How much cooking oil does your family use? A lot of cooking oil has to be put into deep fat fryers. If your family uses a deep fat fryer, make a note of how often the oil is replaced. See if you can make the oil last longer by draining the oil through a piece of kitchen paper to remove any bits of food.

What do you do with the old cooking oil? Oil should not be tipped down the drain as it could block pipes. Small quantities of oil can be mixed into a compost heap. Large quantities should be placed in an old plastic bottle and placed in the bin.

Some recycling centres have containers for waste cooking oil, such as this one in the UK.

Rendering

Waste fat can be collected from places such as restaurants and factories and taken to a rendering plant. Here the oil is cleaned to remove all the bits of food. The different oils are mixed together and sold to other manufacturers who use it to make soap, cosmetics and skincare products.

Did you know...?

In some countries, such as the UK, about 100,000 tonnes of waste oil is produced each year.

Animal additives and fuels

Oil contains a lot of energy and so some of the reclaimed oil is used as an additive for animal food. The oil in the food helps farm animals to put on weight.

There are specialist oil-recycling companies who convert cooking oil into a fuel for vehicles. Cooking oil is extracted from the seeds of crop plants such as oilseed rape. This means the fuel comes from a sustainable source as the plants can be regrown each year.

These barrels contain oil that will be recycled and used again. The oil has come from a variety of industries.

Food into fuel

When organic matter such as food rots down it releases gases such as methane. These gases can be collected and burnt as a fuel.

Biogas digesters

In many countries, household and animal waste is tipped into a biogas digester to make a gas for cooking and heating water. A biogas digester is an underground chamber, often made of concrete. Organic waste, such as food and animal droppings, are collected and tipped into the digester. Inside the chamber, the organic matter heats up and micro-organisms break it down and produce a gas. The gas is taken away in pipes and stored in an over-ground container.

On a larger scale, modern biogas digesters can deal with large quantities of food waste, such as spoilt crops and vegetables, that would normally be dumped in a landfill site. The gas from these digesters is usually burnt to produce heat, which is used to generate electricity.

Many homes in India have a small biogas digester outside. Animal and food waste is tipped into the underground container where it rots down and produces biogas.

This is a large commercial biogas digester in Germany. The containers are built above ground. The biogas is collected and piped to local factories where it is burnt to produce heat.

It's my world!

You can see for yourself how gas is produced from decomposing food. Put a small amount of vegetable peelings in a plastic bag and tie the plastic bag so air cannot get out. Leave the bag outside for a week or so and see if the peelings have produced any gas.

Electricity from food waste

Waste food can also be burnt in special waste-to-energy incinerators to produce electricity. Food contains lots of energy-rich substances, such as fats and sugars. When food is burnt it releases heat. This heat can be used to make steam, which is used to turn a turbine and generate electricity.

The way ahead

See if you and your family can cut down on the amount of food and packaging that you throw away each week.

Don't buy too much

Does your family buy more food than is necessary? Does food you have bought often go off and end up in the bin? 'Buy one, get one free' offers are not a good idea if your family cannot eat or store the extra food.

Young people often eat lots of snack foods such as crisps. Not only are crisps and similar foods unhealthy but they come in bags which have to be thrown away.

Don't be greedy

In developed countries the number of people who are overweight is growing rapidly. This is because food is readily available and fatty foods such as biscuits, crisps and chips are cheap. Try not to cook more than you can eat as it will only make you overweight or end up in the bin. Smaller portions of food are better as they are healthier and they cut down on waste.

Some uneaten food can be reheated or made into new food dishes, but remember to reheat it thoroughly to kill any bacteria that may be present. Any vegetable or fruit scraps can go on a compost heap or in a wormery rather than in the bin. However, leftover meat and fish should be wrapped up and thrown away as it attracts rats.

It's my world!

Why not try growing some of your own vegetables? This is a great way to reduce food waste and fun, too. It cuts out all the waste created by the shops, transport and packaging. You can grow them in your garden or even a window box. Any waste from your own vegetables can go straight on a compost heap and the nutrients recycled back to the soil for the next crop.

Buy from markets

Much of our food is transported long distances and this uses up fuel. Often the food requires extra packaging to protect it. There are now many local markets such as farmers' markets where you can buy food that has been grown locally. The food does not need to be transported very far so less fuel is used and there is minimal packaging and waste.

Some farms have fields of fruits and vegetables where people can go to pick their own. This reduces food waste and transport, too.

Carrots are really easy to grow. Other easy-to-grow vegetables include tomatoes, lettuces and courgettes.

Glossary

Bacteria
microscopic single-celled organisms.
Some can cause disease

Biodegradable
able to be broken down naturally by micro-
organisms such as bacteria and fungi

BSE (bovine spongiform encephalopathy)
a brain disease that occurs in cattle, often
called mad cow disease

Compost
to break down waste garden matter.
Compost is a soil-like material that
is full of nutrients

Decomposer
an organism that causes something
to break down, for example fungi

Developed country
a country in which most people have
a high standard of living

Developing country
a country in which most people have a
low standard of living and who have poor
access to goods and services compared
with people in a developed country

Fertilizer
a substance that provides plants with
all the nutrients that they require

Foot-and-mouth
a disease that affects cattle, sheep, pigs
and goats and spreads quickly from one
animal to another

Pollution
the release of harmful materials into the
environment

Recycle
to process and reuse materials in order
to make new items

Reduce
to lower the amount of waste that is
produced

Reuse
to use something again, either in the same
way or in a different way

Sewer
a waste pipe that carries away sewage
from toilets

Sustainable
of a resource that can continue to be
manufactured into the future without
harming the environment

Turbine
a machine with blades that spin when
driven by steam, gas, water or wind

Vermiculture
the cultivation of worms to break down waste

Waste
anything that is thrown away,
abandoned, or released into the
environment in a way that could harm
the environment

Wormery
a container in which to keep worms

Websites

Composting Waste

These two websites give plenty of information about composting garden waste:

www.gnb.ca/0009/0372/0003/
0001-e.asp

www.moea.state.mn.us/campaign/
compost

Food Collection Service

www.ealing.gov.uk/services/environment/
recycling/new+food+waste+collection+
service+.asp
Learn how some areas of London are setting up a food collection service.

Food Scrap Management in California

www.ciwmb.ca.gov/FoodWaste/
Website looking at how California deals with 5 million tonnes of food scraps each year and ways that this can be reduced.

How To Be a Gardener

www.bbc.co.uk/gardening/htbg/module7/
growing_vegetables.shtml
Website with lots of information about growing your own vegetables.

Recycle Now

www.recyclenow.com/index.html
Really useful UK website covering recycling at home, in the garden, at work, at school, at the shops and at leisure.

United States Environment Protection Agency

www.epa.gov/epaoswer/osw/citizens.htm
Webpages showing how everybody living in the USA can help to reduce the amount of waste that is produced.

This URL takes you to a page that tells you about food: www.epa.gov/epaoswer/
non-hw/reduce/food/food.htm

Waste Online

www.wasteonline.org.uk
Comprehensive website looking at all aspects of recycling.

Waste Wise for Kids: Worms Against Waste

www.gould.edu.au/wastewise/kids/
activity_02.htm
Australian webpage that shows you how to build your own wormery.

Every effort has been made by the publisher to ensure that these websites are suitable for children and contain no inappropriate or offensive material. However, because of the nature of the internet it is impossible to guarantee that the contents of these sites will not be altered. We strongly advise that internet access is supervised by a responsible adult.

Index